Welcome to the White House, Madam President!

With the Presidential Playset, you can draft executive orders in the Oval Office, deliver stirring speeches on the White House lawn, and take decisive action in the Situation Room.

Turn the pages to pick the perfect outfit and add your favorite fashion accessories. Mix and mingle with distinguished guests, blow Bill a kiss while he putters about the lawn, and tangle with all kinds of Republican adversaries. Oh, and be on the lookout for those pesky White House ghosts!

To assemble your playset, wrap the elastic band around both the front cover and White House set (as shown in step 3).

MADAM PRESIDENT

Customize your Hillary Clinton doll with the expression of your choice. Then turn the page for more pantsuits and fashion accessories!

BADASS

Dignified Disapproval

As If!

Commander in Chief

Red Carpet Ready!

Scholarly

PRESIDENTIAL PANTSUITS

Suit up for your daily duties in these classic all-business separate sets!

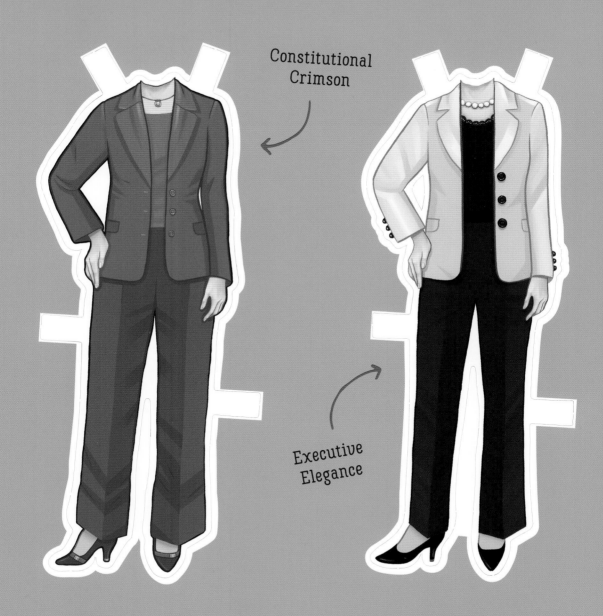

Constitutional Crimson

Executive Elegance

FORMALWEAR AND SLEEPWEAR

Dress for after-hours success in an elegant state dinner gown. Or get cozy for power-naptime in White House jammies.

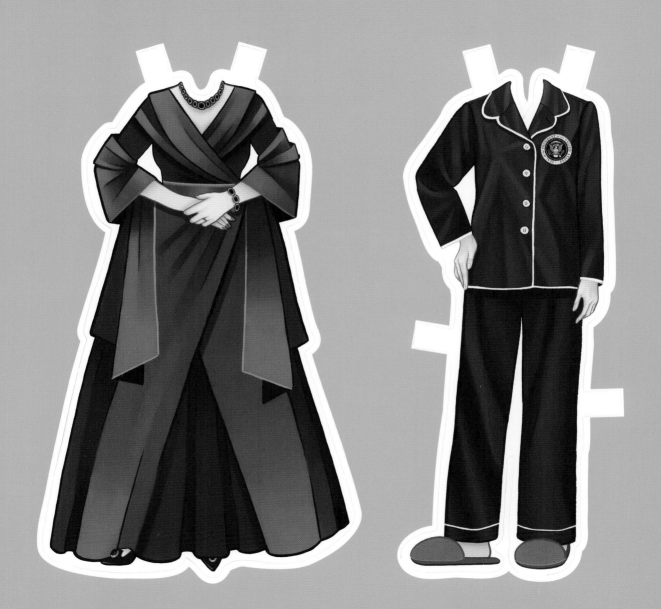

SECRET SERVICE BODYGUARDS

It takes a village to protect POTUS. Madam President never travels without the necessary safeguards. Sometimes Liberty even rides on her shoulder!

Agent Grant

Liberty the Eagle

Constitutional Shield

We the People

THE FIRST GENTLEMAN

Bill keeps up appearances by tending the White House lawn, and still serenades Madam President with his saxophone.

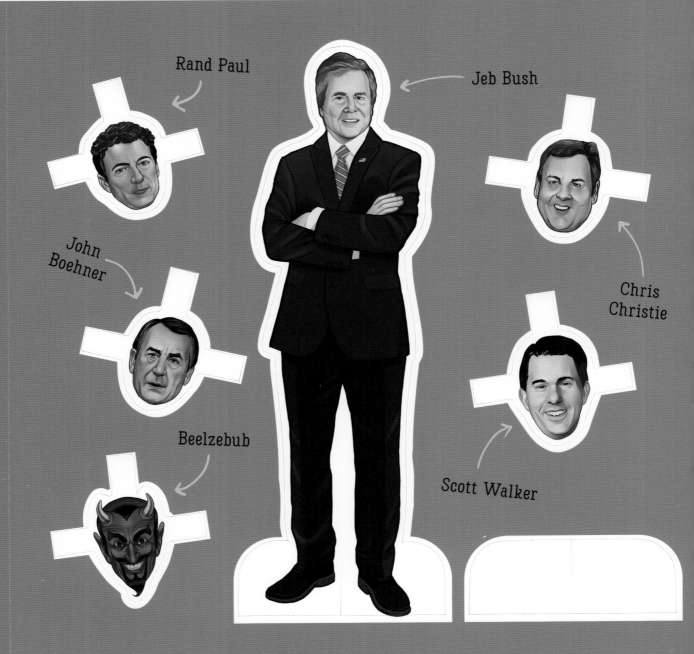

REPUBLICAN ADVERSARIES

Stay tough but polite with your opponents as you debate today's most controversial issues!

Rand Paul

Jeb Bush

John Boehner

Chris Christie

Beelzebub

Scott Walker

TRUSTED POLITICAL ADVISORS

Take time for a tête-à-tête with two of the world's eminent policy experts.

Bono

Oprah Winfrey

SUPREME COURT JUSTICES

They'll check and balance all of your important decisions—so extend them some supreme courtesy!

Clarence Thomas

Ruth Bader Ginsburg

WHITE HOUSE GHOSTS

Boo...who? When forced to make a difficult decision, take time to commune with these friendly White House phantoms!

Jacqueline Kennedy Onassis

George Washington

Amelia Earhart

Eleanor Roosevelt

Abraham Lincoln

Nancy Reagan

THE SEAT OF POWER

Once you've assembled this desk, place it in the Oval Office, then get ready to sign some executive orders. You're in charge!

fold down top of desk along front edge

fold side panel here

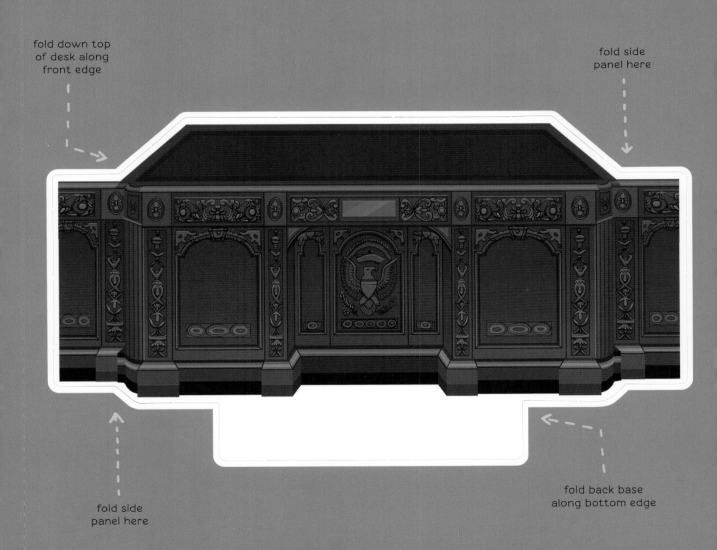

fold side panel here

fold back base along bottom edge

THE BULLY PULPIT

Once you've assembled this podium, carry it out to the White House lawn and address your fellow Americans. Remember, it's never too early to start running for your second term!

fold side panel here

fold side panel here

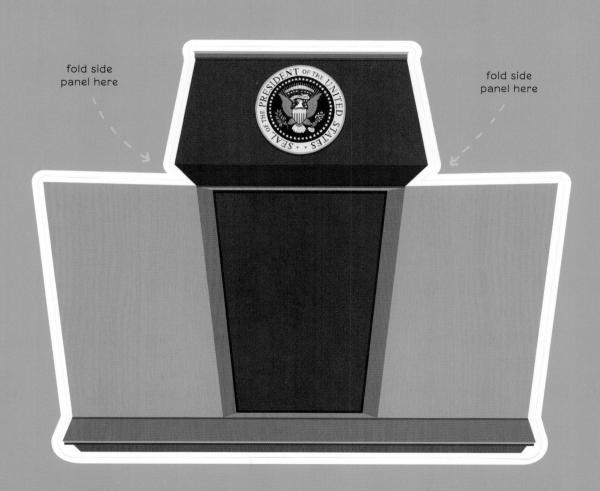